ENGLISH
Practice
Questions

Gillian Howell
Updated by Madeleine Barnes
Series Editor: Richard Cooper

Rising Stars UK Ltd, 7 Hatchers Mews, Bermondsey Street, London SE1 3GS

www.risingstars-uk.com

All facts are correct at time of going to press.

First published 2003
Second edition 2008
Third edition 2010
This edition 2014

First edition written by: Richard Cooper
Second edition written by: Gillian Howell
Third edition updated by: Madeleine Barnes
Educational consultant: Lorna Pepper
Fourth edition educational consultant: Maria Richards
Project management and editorial: Bruce Nicholson
Illustrations: Phill Burrows, Clive Wakfer and Julian Baker
Design: Clive Sutherland
Cover design: Burville-Riley Partnership

Acknowledgements
p46 Extract from *Kensuke's Kingdom* by Michael Morpurgo *(Egmont, 2005)*; p50-51 *Extract based on material from Eagle and birds of prey* by Jemima Parry-Jones (Dorling Kindersley, 2000); p53-54 Reproduced with kind permission of Shannon Thunderbird, www.shannonthunderbird.com

Every effort has been made to trace copyright holders and obtain their permission for the use of copyright material. The authors and publishers will gladly receive information enabling them to rectify any error or omission in subsequent editions.

British Library Cataloguing in Publication Data
A CIP record for this book is available from the British Library.

ISBN 978-1-78339-411-1

Printed by Craft Print International Ltd., Singapore

Contents

How to use this book   4

About the National Tests   6

Writing non-fiction   8

Writing fiction   14

Grammar   24

Punctuation   28

Vocabulary   34

Spelling   38

Reviewing your work   42

Writing and reading skills   43

Reading comprehension   44

The answers can be found in a pull-out section
in the middle of this book.

How to use this book

Writing non-fiction (pages 8–13)

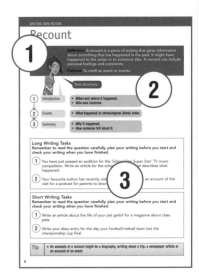

(1) **Definition** and **Purpose** – Helps you to understand what this type of writing is for and how it is used.

(2) **Text structure** – Flow chart that describes the key elements of the text type, step by step.

(3) **Independent writing** – This gives further opportunities for writing long and short pieces of a similar style.

Writing fiction (pages 14–23)

✷ Introduction to classic story structure.

✷ Also provides advice and practice questions so you can master the key features of fiction writing, including settings and character descriptions.

✷ Useful planning grids are included on pages 18–23 for each genre of fiction. There are also lots of independent writing tasks for you to complete.

Practising grammar for non-fiction writing (pages 24–27)

(1) Description of the main types of grammar for non-fiction writing, including dos and don'ts.

(2) Practice questions to help you to master these important features of writing.

Additional support

Punctuation (pages 28–33)
A range of exercises covering key Level 4 punctuation; includes work on the use of ellipses, dashes and semi-colons. It also includes a quick punctuation test.

Vocabulary (pages 34–37)
These vocabulary exercises focus on improving your writing by making sure that 'every word counts'. Each section has a brief explanation, followed by exercises in developing and using Level 4 vocabulary.

Spelling practice (pages 38–41)
These exercises are designed to give useful practice in the more difficult areas of spelling – plurals, tenses and common errors.

Reviewing your work (page 42)
Supportive notes on how to continually review your writing and develop your handwriting skills.

Reading comprehension (pages 43–56)

(1) **The text** – A range of texts are given, including fiction, non-fiction and poetry.

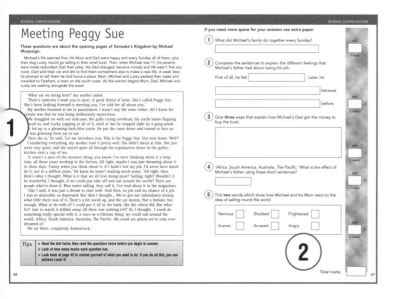

(2) **The questions** – Comprehension questions that allow you to demonstrate your Level 4 skills. The number of marks available is given and there is space to write your answers.

About the National Tests

Key facts

* The Key Stage 2 National Tests take place in the summer term in Year 6. You will be tested on Maths and English.

* The tests take place in your school and will be marked by examiners – not your teacher!

* Individual test scores are not made public but a school's combined scores are published in what are commonly known as 'league tables'.

The National Tests for English

You will take three tests in English. These are designed to test your reading comprehension, grammar, punctuation and spelling. Your writing is now teacher assessed, along with handwriting.

The Reading Test

This is one test to assess your reading comprehension. In this test you will be given a series of texts and an answer booklet. You will have one hour to read the texts and complete the answer booklet section of the test. You use the texts to answer the questions so you do not need to memorise them. You should refer to the texts closely while you are answering. Some of the questions guide you to a particular page, 'Look at page 6,' but you will need to identify the correct text in other questions.

The Grammar, Punctuation and Spelling Test

The grammar and punctuation part of the test lasts 45 minutes. There are different types of questions for you to answer in different ways. For some questions you do not need to do any writing. Instead, they are multiple choice options, ticking the correct answer, drawing lines to, or putting a circle around your answers. It is incredibly important therefore to read the instructions carefully, so that you know how to answer the question. For other questions however, you will need to write a word, phrase or sentence.

The spelling task lasts 15 minutes, although you will be allowed as much time as you need to complete it. Your teacher or another adult will read out twenty sentences. Each sentence has a word missing in the answer booklet. You must listen carefully to the missing word and fill this in, making sure that you spell it correctly. The word will be read out once, then as part of a sentence and then repeated a third and final time.

Recount

Definition A recount is a piece of writing that gives information about something that has happened in the past. It might have happened to the writer or to someone else. A recount can include personal feelings and comments.

Purpose To retell an event or events.

Text structure

1 Introduction
- *When* and *where* it happened.
- *Who* was involved.

2 Events
- *What* happened in chronological (time) order.

3 Summary
- *Why* it happened.
- *How* someone felt about it.

Long Writing Tasks
Remember to read the question carefully, plan your writing before you start and check your writing when you have finished.

1 You have just passed an audition for the 'School Star Super Star' TV music competition. Write an article for the school magazine that describes what happened.

2 Your favourite author has recently visited your school. Write an account of the visit for a podcast for parents to download.

Short Writing Tasks
Remember to read the question carefully, plan your writing before you start and check your writing when you have finished.

1 Write an article about the life of your pet gerbil for a magazine about class pets.

2 Write your diary entry for the day your football/netball team lost the championship cup final.

Tip	★ An example of a recount might be a biography, writing about a trip, a newspaper article or an account of an event.

Instructions and procedures

Definition Instructions tell a reader how to do, make or play something, or how to get somewhere.

Purpose To instruct.

Text structure

1	Aim	This is the title and tells a reader what the instructions are about.
2	What you need	A list of the things needed to achieve the aim. These are listed in order of use.
3	What you do	A step-by-step chronological (time order) sequence of what to do to achieve the aim.

Long Writing Tasks
Remember to read the question carefully, plan your writing before you start and check your writing when you have finished.

1 Write a detailed set of instructions to tell a visitor from another planet how to get from your house to your school. Remember, he or she knows nothing about traffic!

2 You are going away for the weekend but you need a friend to look after your rare and dangerous plant, 'the poison-spitting chrysotum', in your greenhouse. Write a set of instructions to help him or her keep your plant alive.

Short Writing Tasks
Remember to read the question carefully, plan your writing before you start and check your writing when you have finished.

1 Your elderly neighbour has bought a mobile phone for the first time but it had no instructions with it. Write a set of instructions about how to use the menu features so that he can send text messages.

2 Write an email to a friend to tell him or her how to join an online 'friends' website.

Tip	★ Instructions can be in the form of recipes, rules for playing a game, pictures or directions. Remember to think about the purpose of the writing!

Non-chronological report

Definition Non-chronological reports give a reader information about something or somewhere. They are usually about a group of things (e.g. *dinosaurs*), not one thing in particular (e.g. *Dilly the dinosaur*). Facts about the subject are organised into paragraphs.

Purpose To give information.

(1) Title   Text structure

(2) Introduction   **Definition of the subject.**

(3) Series of paragraphs about various aspects of the subject   **Facts usually grouped by topic.**

(4) Summary or a rounding-off statement   **Could be an unusual fact about the subject.**

Long Writing Tasks
Remember to read the question carefully, plan your writing before you start and check your writing when you have finished.

(1) Write a report about the playground games and other activities that take place during the lunch hour at your school. Organise the activities into alphabetical order in your report.

(2) Write a report about clothes you wear for different occasions. Describe the different types of clothing: boys' clothes, girls' clothes and summer/winter differences.

Short Writing Tasks
Remember to read the question carefully, plan your writing before you start and check your writing when you have finished.

(1) Write a report about the programmes children watch on television.

(2) Write notes for a report about the subjects studied at your school.

Tip	★ **Reports can be in the form of letters, encyclopaedia entries, information posters or leaflets, as well as straightforward pieces of writing.**
	A non-chronological report on a school might include headings such as:
	• Number of pupils • After-school clubs • Location
	Remember to think about the purpose of your writing!

Explanation

Definition An explanation tells the reader how or why something works or happens. It can be about natural things (e.g. *How lakes are formed*), or about mechanical things (e.g. *How a telephone works*).

Purpose To explain.

Text structure

1	Title	Tells the reader what the explanation is about. Often contains *how* or *why*.
2	Introduction	Definition of the subject of the explanation.
3	A paragraph describing the parts and/or appearance of the subject or process to be explained
4	A paragraph explaining what something does, or why or how it works, often in time order
5	Concluding paragraph	Could include where the subject can be found or what it is used for.

Long Writing Tasks
Remember to read the question carefully, plan your writing before you start and check your writing when you have finished.

1 Write an explanation about the process of keeping your bedroom tidy, which you share with a very untidy younger brother or sister.

2 You think you have a great way of re-organising your cluttered classroom. Write an explanation for your teacher to explain why your way will be better.

Short Writing Tasks
Remember to read the question carefully, plan your writing before you start and check your writing when you have finished.

1 You have been asked to run in the school marathon. Write an explanation about why you do not want to take part.

2 Draw a flow chart to explain what happens when torrential rain makes a river flood.

| Tip | ★ Explanations can be in the form of letters, diagrams, information leaflets, encyclopaedia entries and posters. |

Discussion

Definition A discussion text, or *balanced argument*, gives the reader information about an issue from different points of view. Readers are then left to make up their mind about how they feel about the issue.

Purpose To present opposing points of view about an issue.

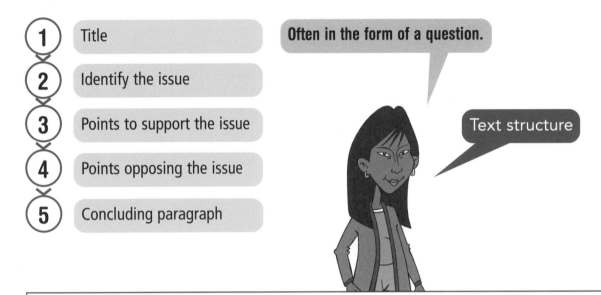

1. Title — Often in the form of a question.
2. Identify the issue
3. Points to support the issue
4. Points opposing the issue — Text structure
5. Concluding paragraph

Long Writing Tasks
Remember to read the question carefully, plan your writing before you start and check your writing when you have finished.

1. 'Children should be allowed to use the Internet to help them do tests for school.' Write the arguments for and against.

2. 'Children should not be allowed to have their own mobile phones.' Write the arguments for and against.

Short Writing Tasks
Remember to read the question carefully, plan your writing before you start and check your writing when you have finished.

1. Write a paragraph to summarise the advantages and disadvantages of having compulsory school sports every Saturday morning.

2. Write an opening paragraph to discuss/describe the issues for and against building a big new supermarket on the outskirts of your town or village.

Tip	★ You might be asked to write an account in the form of a newspaper or magazine article. Remember to back up your ideas with evidence.

Persuasion

Definition A persuasive text tries to make the reader think, do or buy something.

Purpose To persuade.

Text structure

1 Identify the main point of the text

2 Reasons to support the point, organised into paragraphs

3 Summary of the key points

4 Call to action

Long Writing Tasks
Remember to read the question carefully, plan your writing before you start and check your writing when you have finished.

1 Write a speech to persuade your school governors that there should be a pupil representative, who could help the governors to make important decisions about the school, and that you would be perfect for the job.

2 The school that you attend does not have a school-crossing patrol. Write a letter to convince the local council that you need a safe crossing place for the pupils.

Short Writing Tasks
Remember to read the question carefully, plan your writing before you start and check your writing when you have finished.

1 You are trying to raise money for charity by dyeing your hair purple. Design a poster to encourage people to sponsor you.

2 You have found an escaped pet snake in your house. Write an advertisement for the local newspaper to persuade the owner or anyone else to take it away.

Story structure

All stories are organised in the same basic way.

When you plan and write, think in five sections.

(1) **Beginning**
Introduce the **main characters** and the **setting**.

(2) **Build-up**
The **story gets going** – the characters start to do something.

(3) **Problem**
Something goes wrong for the characters. This is the most exciting part.

(4) **Resolution**
The **problem is sorted** out in some way.

(5) **Ending**
All the **loose ends are tied up**. The characters **reflect on (think about)** what happened.

Think of some stories you know or have read recently. Do they fit this pattern?

Setting, characters and theme

Before even planning a story, you need to decide on the three main ingredients.

Setting

This is WHEN and WHERE the story takes place. You need to help readers to make pictures in their minds. The setting can also be used to create an atmosphere and affect how the reader feels.

Think about some stories you have read. When and where were they set? How do you know? Look at some short stories to see how the authors have told the reader about the setting. Have a go at drawing the setting that you read about.

Characters

This is WHO is in the story. You need to help the reader build up a picture of the main characters. They need to have an idea of what the characters are like.

Think about some stories you have read. Who were the characters? What were they like? How do you know? What were they called? Look at some short stories to see how authors have told the reader about the characters. Try drawing a character as you see them.

Theme

This is WHAT happens in the story. Some people say that there are only a few story themes in the world. All writers borrow ideas from other stories, and this is something you can do.

Think about some stories you have read. What happened? Did one story remind you of any others? List some of the common themes, e.g. good overcoming evil, main character losing something.

Once you've chosen your ingredients, mix them together and make a story!

Let's practise!

Pages 16–23 give you plenty of practice at developing your fiction writing skills.

Page 16: Choose an idea to develop a paragraph about setting.

Page 17: Choose an idea to develop a paragraph about a character.

Pages 18–23: These are independent writing tasks on a range of themes (e.g. adventure story, science-fiction tale, mystery story). Planning sheets are included to help you plan your writing.

WHAT   WHO   WHEN   WHERE

Make sure you practise all these pages to help you achieve a Level 4 for your writing!

Setting

Use one of the ideas below to develop a paragraph about a setting. The answer section contains a model answer for the first setting. It is longer than you would be expected to write but will give you ideas for future writing.

(1) A gust of wind shook the branches and cold drops of water fell on Mark's face as he peered up into the overhanging trees. Where could the cat have gone?

(2) Rifat leant back against the shop window and slowly got her breath back. Unconcerned shoppers streamed past her, their hands gripping large carrier bags and their faces concentrating on getting to the next bargain.

(3) As the ship slowly descended, the landscape became clearer. Lucas could just make out an irregular surface that seemed to be covered in a dark grey dusty powder.

(4) At last the bottom of the boat scraped on solid ground and stopped. The breakers tried to toss it further up the shore but it stuck fast. As they stepped onto the island, everyone looked around.

(5) The lift clanked to a stop and Maria stepped out with the others. The only light came from the beams of the torches on their helmets. Maria was shocked by how hot she suddenly felt.

Characters

Use one of the ideas below to develop a paragraph about a character. The answer section contains a model answer for the first character. It is longer than you would be expected to write but will give you ideas for future writing.

(1) The story is about a small village from long ago. One old man in the village is thought to have special powers and great wisdom. Write a description of what he looks like and how he moves as seen by a young girl.

(2) You are about to present a bouquet to the Mayoress at the opening of a new school. Describe how she looks and how you feel about her.

(3) Introduce the main character of a story about a boy who is being bullied on the way home from school.

(4) Mrs Jolly owns the local sweet shop. Write a character description about her.

(5) Jacob is in a bank when it is held up. Write a description of the leader of the gang of robbers.

_____

_____

_____

_____

_____

_____

_____

_____

_____

_____

_____

_____

_____

_____

Adventure story

Example: *James and the Giant Peach*

Use the planning sheet below to help you complete one of the independent writing tasks.

You can draw your own planning sheets using the headings below.

Beginning Introduce the main characters and the setting.	
Build-up The story gets going – the characters start to do something.	
Problem Something goes wrong for the characters. This is the most exciting point.	
Resolution The problem is resolved in some way.	
Ending The loose ends are tied up. The characters reflect on (think about) what happened.	

Independent writing
Plan and write your own adventure story using one of these titles.
1. The Amazon Expedition
2. The Curse of the Green Diamond
3. Smugglers' Inn
4. Jack and the Missing Medals
5. Marooned in Space
6. The Race to the Pole
7. Carly Gets Gold!

Myths and legends

Example: *King Arthur and the Knights of the Round Table*

Use the planning sheet below to help you complete one of the independent writing tasks.

You can draw your own planning sheets using the headings below.

Beginning Set the scene. Introduce the main characters, especially the hero, and the setting. Note down words to use to show the *time* when the myth or legend is set.	
Build-up Add information about what the characters' aims, hopes or desires are and why. Introduce any elements of magic that are needed for the myth or legend.	
Problem Something goes wrong. This is where a villain or accident prevents the hero accomplishing his or her aim.	
Resolution The problem is overcome. This might be through a magical item or a supernatural helper.	
Ending The loose ends are tied up. The main character is often welcomed as a hero or the characters reflect on the events.	

Independent writing
Plan and write your own myth or legend using one of these titles.
1. The First Rainbow
2. The Legend of the Golden Goblet
3. Dora and the Three Dragons
4. Daring Sir Duncan
5. Why it Snows in Winter
6. The Legend of the Last Unicorn
7. How Tiger got his Stripes

Traditional tale

Example: *Little Red Riding Hood*

Use the planning sheet below to help you complete one of the independent writing tasks.

You can draw your own planning sheets using the headings below.

Beginning Set the scene. Introduce the main characters and the setting.	
Build-up Add information about the characters. Think of using three events (e.g. Three Little Pigs – house of straw/wood/bricks; Goldilocks – three bears; she tries the porridge/chairs/bed three times).	
Problem Something goes wrong. This is the most exciting part.	
Resolution The problem is overcome.	
Ending The loose ends are tied up. The main character often learns a lesson.	

Independent writing
Plan and write your own traditional tale using one of these titles.
1. Princess Emerald and the Three Frogs
2. The Story of Jack the Joker
3. Princess Big Nose
4. The Cowardly Lion
5. The Magic Necklace
6. The Boy who Wished to Grow Up
7. Jacob and the Little Donkey

Modern story

Example: *The Story of Tracey Beaker*

Use the planning sheet below to help you complete one of the independent writing tasks.

You can draw your own planning sheets using the headings below.

Beginning Introduce the main characters and the setting.	
Build-up The story gets going – the characters start to do something.	
Problem Something goes wrong for the characters. This is the most exciting point.	
Resolution The problem is resolved in some way.	
Ending The loose ends are tied up. The characters reflect on (think about) what happened.	

Independent writing
Plan and write your own modern story using one of these titles.
1. Robocat to the Rescue!
2. Sally the Skateboard Star
3. Three Gifts for Gareth
4. Lost in the Shopping Mall
5. Don't Do It, Dave!
6. My Mum's an Astronaut
7. The Tyrannical Teacher

Science fiction tale

Example: The *Artemis Fowl* series

Use the planning sheet below to help you complete one of the independent writing tasks.

You can draw your own planning sheets using the headings below.

Beginning Set the scene. Introduce the main characters and the setting. The setting is important as it will tell readers what sort of story to expect.	
Build-up Add information about the characters and what they do in the setting. Here you can introduce stranger characters, aliens and unusual life-forms.	
Problem Something goes wrong. This is the most exciting part.	
Resolution The problem is overcome.	
Ending The loose ends are tied up. The characters think about what has happened.	

Independent writing
Plan and write your own science fiction tale using one of these titles.
1. My Mum's an Alien
2. Invasion of the Androids
3. The Race around the Red Planet
4. The Future Car
5. Our Teacher comes from Outer Space
6. My Homework Machine
7. Moving to the Moon

Mystery story

Example: *The London Eye Mystery* by Siobhan Dowd

Use the planning sheet below to help you complete one of the independent writing tasks.

You can draw up your own planning sheets using the headings below.

Beginning Set the scene. Introduce the main characters (those who will solve the mystery) and the setting.	
Build-up Add information about the characters and what they do in the setting. Here you can lull your reader into thinking everything is normal.	
Problem Now something goes wrong which is unexplainable. Here you can add clues to get the reader thinking.	
Resolution The main character or characters find answers to the clues and solve the mystery.	
Ending The clues are all explained and the reader gets to understand how the main characters solved the mystery. There might be a lesson learned or a moral.	

Independent writing

Plan and write your own mystery story using one of these titles.

1. The Mystery of the Missing Homework
2. The Lost Treasure of the Town Museum
3. Where's Max?
4. The School Detective Agency
5. The Disappearance of the Championship Cup
6. Wrongly Accused!
7. The Poisoned Pineapple

Tip	★ Remember to keep your planning notes short, just the key words to remind you about setting, characters and what is going on.

Grammar

Achieve Level 4 writing

At Level 4, your writing is lively and thoughtful. You can develop your ideas and organise them according to the purpose of your writing. You can make adventurous choices of vocabulary and use words for effect. You can use complex sentences, and your spelling and punctuation is usually accurate. Your handwriting is fluent, joined and legible.

The passive voice or impersonal writing

Most information texts use formal, impersonal language. Avoid using first and second person pronouns *I* and *you*. Passive verbs can give your writing a more formal tone but don't overdo it. Using too many passive verbs can make your writing difficult to read and sound stiff. Use a balance of passive and active verbs.

Examples:

Active: *John drank the whole glass.*   Passive: *The whole glass was drunk by John.*

Active: *A passing ship rescued them.*   Passive: *They were rescued by a passing ship.*

Rewrite these paragraphs using a more formal tone. Use extra paper if you need to.

1 Skateboarders can sometimes make other people concerned. They whizz along the pavement and can cause accidents. Skateboarders should always use the special parks that are set aside for them.

_____

_____

_____

2 You can find monkeys in many different countries around the world. You can see Colobus monkeys in many parts of the African continent. Macaque monkeys you see in Africa and Asia.

_____

_____

_____

3 When you want to be sure of making a good meal, it is a good idea to find a good recipe first. Read the recipe and then get the ingredients that you are going to need.

_____

_____

_____

Formal descriptions

Rewrite these sentences using a more formal description.

1 Ferrari cars are fast, sleek and good-looking. Many people would love to drive a Ferrari but can't afford one because they cost a lot of money. Ferraris are usually red or yellow and have a badge called a prancing pony.

_____

_____

_____

_____

2 If you found a lost kitten, you would probably fall in love with its cute big eyes and tiny fluffy body. Then, when it licked your face with its rough little tongue, you would probably want to keep it forever. But the best thing you could do for it is to try to find out where it came from.

_____

_____

_____

_____

3 The cakes on the counter range from plain buns to fancy cakes. There are buns with snowy white icing and a glistening red cherry in the middle and cakes with scrummy chocolate icing and masses of hundreds-and-thousands scattered all over.

_____

_____

_____

_____

4 When he saw the crowd, the policeman quickly made a note. He wrote, 'A big crowd of brightly dressed people has gathered in the road. They seem to be singing rather tunelessly but very noisily.'

_____

_____

_____

_____

Simple present tense

Rewrite these sentences in the simple present tense. Use extra paper if needed.

(1) In the summer, many people experienced the flooding of their homes. The water rose so quickly that they lost their belongings.

_____

_____

(2) Although matches in the old stadium were popular, many more people went to see the games in the new stadium.

_____

_____

(3) The traffic was very heavy. The jam that resulted stretched for ten miles.

_____

_____

Using verbs in fiction

Rewrite these sentences using more interesting choices of verbs.

(1) Matt sighed as he <u>looked</u> out of the window at the lines of cars <u>going</u> into the distance.

_____

_____

(2) Sam <u>ran</u> through the meadow.

_____

_____

(3) 'Nobody understands me!' she said <u>sadly</u>.

_____

_____

Connectives

Complete these sentences using connectives. More than one connective fits each sentence. Choose the one that fits the best.

1 [ ] you play the game you will enjoy it. [ ] if you

decide to cheat no one will enjoy it.

2 [ ] collect together three sheets of A4 card, some sticky tape and

crayons. [ ] fold the card so the corners meet in the middle.

3 [ ] four people gather together they are a group.

[ ] if more than ten gather together they are classed as a crowd.

4 [ ] the weather has been sunny for a few weeks, it might still rain.

[ ] it would have to rain very heavily to avoid a drought.

5 [ ] the boat shuddered violently. [ ] the children

saw the shark's menacing fin break the surface.

6 [ ] the tide was coming in quickly, he still felt he had time to explore.

[ ] he knew he didn't have long before he had to return home.

7 [ ] it was over. [ ] everything that had happened

we were safe.

Tip	★ These are just *some* of the connectives you could use. See which ones are best for the sentences.			
	However	*Although*	*Only*	*Just then*
	Though	*Nevertheless*	*If*	*But*
	So	*Despite*	*Also*	*Because*
	All at once	*Suddenly*	*At last*	*Therefore*

Punctuation

Punctuation allows you to mark your writing so that the reader knows how to read it.

Capital letters and full stops

- Every sentence should start with a capital letter and end with a full stop (.), question mark (?) or exclamation mark (!).
- Names of people, places, days of the week and months of the year all start with a capital letter. Initial letters used for people's names (e.g. H G Wells) or organisations (e.g. NASA) are always written in capital letters. The seasons – spring, summer, autumn and winter – do *not* begin with capital letters.

Can you rewrite these sentences using the correct punctuation?

1 matt thought london was very noisy and crowded

2 majid enjoyed playing football but was never picked for the team

3 she wanted polly to visit on saturday

4 jon thinks mrs singh is a great teacher

5 j k rowling is the author of the harry potter stories

6 hamburgers are very popular in america

7 next summer we are visiting s e asia

8 jacob and rose were both born in huddersfield

ENGLISH

Answers for
Practice Questions

Page 16 – Writing fiction – Setting

A gust of wind shook the branches and cold drops of water fell on Mark's face as he peered up into the overhanging trees. Where could the cat have gone? Mark's eyes searched quickly through the dark bare branches of tree after tree but saw no sign.

The wood was eerily quiet. There wasn't the slightest rustle of movement in the undergrowth or the sound of birdsong; only the whoosh of wind through the branches for a few moments and then silence fell.

Mark quickly moved between the trees as the sun sank below the horizon and a gloomy twilight descended. He was finding it harder to search the wood as the light faded, but where was the cat? It can't have just disappeared.

The leaves on the ground were wet after the earlier unexpected downpour and muffled Mark's footsteps, so he felt enveloped in a strange silent world where he was the only living being. At last he stood still, listening. At first there was nothing. Then he heard it. A faint mewing in the distance.

Page 17 – Writing fiction – Character descriptions

Old Jacob was sitting on a wooden chair near the entrance to the smithy. His white hair was thin and straggly. Sarah unconsciously ran her fingers through her own thick brown locks. He lifted his face as she approached and squinted in the light, making his face look like crumpled white parchment. Slowly and awkwardly, he heaved himself up using his gnarled hands to push himself upwards and out of the chair. As he walked towards her, he seemed to wince with every laboured step, but when he was close to her he bent easily and fluidly until his eyes were level with hers. She could see they were deep blue and clear and held all the knowledge of the world in their depths.

Sample answer for Writing fiction stories (pages 18–23)

This story follows the story structure on page 14 and contains elements of a variety of themes. You will be able to identify the setting and the characters fairly easily. Try to find examples of the different themes, such as Lost or found/Wishing or wanting/Good overcoming evil, which are shown on pages 18–23.

This story is longer than anything you would be expected to write in your tests.

Try rewriting traditional stories and other stories you are familiar with, but keep the length at five or six paragraphs. The story structure should stay the same – Beginning, Build-up, Problem, Resolution, Ending.

Introduction
This story is an adaptation of a traditional Welsh folktale.

Beginning
Huwie's eyes were blue as the summer sky, and his smile lit up his face. He wanted only to play and run and laugh and he hated school. Huwie's mother, though, always sent him off to school every day.

Build-up
One morning, Huwie set off to school with dragging feet. Halfway there he stopped and sat on the ground, where the sunlight gleamed against the rocks on the hillside. He leant back, and closing his eyes, turned his face up towards the sun. Soon, the warmth, the drone of insects and the birdsong soothed Huwie into sleep.

When he woke, he felt chilled. The light was no longer bright and clear and the sun seemed to be hidden in a twilight mist.

'Have I slept all day?' thought Huwie.

His heart began to thud, for he knew his teachers would be doubly angry with him the next day. Quickly, he leapt to his feet, and was about to run down the hillside to his home, when he heard a strange sound … a light, sparkling sound, like tinkling bells, or water running over pebbles. He stood and listened, his head leaning to one side to catch the faint noise.

'No, not bells,' he said aloud, 'it is laughter!'

Huwie peered behind the boulder. Two strange little people stood there, their shoulders jiggling up and down with their laughter. Huwie began to smile at them, and soon he was laughing with them. They laughed so hard that tears came to his eyes.

The two little people began throwing a shining golden ball to each other, and then to Huwie, and he joined in their game. He laughed and jumped with delight as the ball spun and shone. Then suddenly they went to the hillside and beckoned Huwie to follow them. A crack appeared in the rock, and with wide eyes, Huwie entered.

Problem

When Huwie did not come home, time passed with sad slowness for his mother. Then one morning she stood at her door looking up to the hills as she had done each day, when she saw Huwie running down the hill.

'Where have you been?' she cried. Huwie's blue eyes were bright and his smile lit up his face as he told the strange tale.

'Under the hillside live many little people with long fair hair hanging to their shoulders. They love laughter and games. Their king asked me to stay and play with his sons, as they had fallen in love with my bright smile, so I did and was happy. But at last I grew homesick, so I have come back for just two days. Then I'm going back under the hill to play with my new friends.'

Huwie's mother was sad to hear he would leave again, but as he told her more about his time with the little people, she began to ask him about the shining ball of gold. She thought that the golden ball had cast an enchantment on Huwie and kept him away from her. But it might make them rich!

'When you return, hide the golden ball and bring it to me,' she told him. 'I would love to see it.'

Resolution

Huwie went back and spent happy days with the king's sons, until at last, he longed to see his home and his mother once more. The king of the little people told him to stay away no more than two days, for he had also grown to love the smile that lit up their land under the hillside.

Before he left, Huwie played with the king's sons. Then, secretly, he hid the golden ball under his shirt and left the cave. As he ran down the hillside, he thought he could hear the patter of light feet behind him. Quicker and quicker he ran. Still he heard them pattering behind. Faster and faster he ran, all the way to the door of his house. As he approached, his mother opened the door in delight, but just as he was about to run inside, he stumbled and fell. The golden ball spun from his hands and rolled on the ground, glittering brightly in the daylight. At once, two little people with long fair hair ran lightly to the ball, scooped it up and they and the golden ball were gone.

Ending

Huwie wandered the hillsides for many days, searching for the rock and the cave hidden behind it. He listened sadly for the tinkling sound of laughter, but never again did he find his friends. Huwie's smile was not seen for many years, until at last, when he grew to be a man, he enchanted children with his tales of the little people who lived and laughed under the hill, and played with a magical shining golden ball.

Page 24 – Grammar – The passive voice or impersonal writing

1. People can sometimes be concerned about skateboarders. Accidents can be caused by their use on pavements. The special parks set aside for skateboarders should always be used.

2. Monkeys can be found in many different countries around the world. Colobus monkeys can be seen in many parts of the African continent. In Africa and Asia, Macaque monkeys can be seen.

3. To be sure of making a good meal, first find a good recipe. The recipe should be read carefully and the necessary ingredients collected.

Page 25 – Grammar – Formal descriptions

1. Cars manufactured by Ferrari frequently come with red or yellow paintwork and a distinguishing 'prancing pony' badge. Many people would like to own a Ferrari but the cost prohibits it.

2. If you found a lost kitten, the proper course of action would be to try to find where it came from.

3. The cakes on the counter range from plain buns to fancy cakes with a variety of different icings, decorations and flavours.

4. On seeing the crowd, the policeman made a note of people's appearance and behaviour.

Page 26 – Grammar – Simple present tense

1. In the summer, many people experience the flooding of their homes. The water rises so quickly that they lose their belongings.
2. Although matches in the old stadium are popular, many more people go to see the games in the new stadium.
3. The traffic is very heavy. The jam that results stretches for ten miles.

Page 26 – Grammar – Using verbs in fiction

1. Matt sighed as he <u>stared</u> out of the window at the lines of cars <u>disappearing</u> into the distance.
2. Sam <u>sprinted</u> through the meadow.
3. 'Nobody understands me!' she said <u>miserably</u>.

Page 27 – Grammar – Connectives

Suggested answers (connectives in italics):

1. *When* you play the game you will enjoy it. *However* if you decide to cheat no one will enjoy it.
2. *First/Firstly* collect together three sheets of A4 card, some sticky tape and crayons. *Next/Then/Secondly* fold the card so the corners meet in the middle.
3. *When/If* four people gather together they are a group. *But/However* if more than ten gather together they are classed as a crowd.
4. *Although* the weather has been sunny for a few weeks, it might still rain. *But/However* it would have to rain very heavily to avoid a drought.
5. *All at once/Suddenly* the boat shuddered violently. *Suddenly/All at once/Just then* the children saw the shark's menacing fin break the surface.
6. *Although* the tide was coming in quickly, he still felt he had time to explore. *But/Nevertheless* he knew he didn't have long before he had to return home.
7. *At last/Finally* it was over. *Despite* everything that had happened we were safe!

Page 28 – Punctuation – Capital letters and full stops

1. Matt thought London was very noisy and crowded.
2. Majid enjoyed playing football but was never picked for the team.
3. She wanted Polly to visit on Saturday.
4. Jon thinks Mrs Singh is a great teacher.
5. J K Rowling is the author of the Harry Potter stories.
6. Hamburgers are very popular in America.
7. Next summer we are visiting S E Asia.
8. Jacob and Rose were both born in Huddersfield.

Page 29 – Punctuation – Commas

1. Broccoli, cabbage, spinach and carrots are all full of vitamins.
2. A simple healthy snack can be a few nuts, seeds, raw vegetables or fruit.
3. For a delicious healthy drink, mix some squeezed raspberries, blueberries and a banana with some yoghurt or milk.
4. Some foods contain a lot of fat, salt or sugar, so remember to eat them in moderation.

Page 30 – Punctuation – Speech punctuation

'Have you seen my glasses?' called Granny from the sitting room.

I could just hear her voice so I called back, 'Did you say something, Granny?'

I went downstairs to find out. 'What did you say?' I asked.

'I can't find my glasses,' she replied, 'Will you help me find them? It's such a nuisance.'

'Granny dear!' I laughed, 'Look in the mirror. They're on your head.'
'Oh, silly me!' she laughed.

Pages 31–32 – Punctuation – Apostrophes
1. P
2. O
3. P
4. O
5. O

1. Donna's shoes were covered in mud.
2. Take your chairs and put them in Mr Brown's classroom.
3. The parrot's feathers were blue and red.
4. The soldiers' boots were highly polished.
5. The sailor's clothes were crumpled.

1. I can't finish my story yet.
2. You haven't been swimming for ages.
3. Your mum wouldn't like to see you looking so grubby.
4. This skateboard hasn't got alloy wheels.
5. Tom isn't a good runner.

Can't you make a louder noise than that?

Page 33 – Punctuation – Test your punctuation
The children made a lot of noise as they approached through the wood.
  'We're tramping through the woods,' they sang, 'We're tramping through the fields.' Their voices let us know they were coming so we built up the camp fire and began to heat up the beans and sausages. We knew they would be hungry after the hike.
  'Here you are at last!' I shouted as soon as the first boy, who I think was called Daniel, appeared through the trees, quickly followed by four others. They looked bedraggled but happy.
  'Did you enjoy that?' I asked.
  'Yeah!' they all yelled, 'It was great!'
  Soon Frank Jenkins appeared, bringing up the rear. He beckoned to me and muttered solemnly in my ear, 'I'm afraid there's been a problem.'

Pages 34–35 – Vocabulary – Mind your language
Answers will vary.

Page 36 – Vocabulary – Nouns and verbs
Answers will vary.

Page 36 – Vocabulary – Adjectives
Suggested answers:

Happy mood	Sad mood	Scary mood
smiling, bright, carefree	glum, miserable, tearful	black, angry, white
joyful, uplifting, lively	mumbling, monotonous, sorrowful	threatening, angry, sharp
gentle, caressing, loving	careless, casual, gloomy	icy, cold, angry
warm, gentle, light	rough, cold, bitter	sudden, chilling, sharp

Page 37 – Vocabulary – Adverbs

Answers will vary.

Page 37 – Vocabulary – Alliteration

Suggested answers:

The tall/towering trees were whipped by the wind.

Her toxic/taunting tongue spat out the words.

She hardly heard the sound.

Kurt suddenly strode across the room.

Page 47 – Reading comprehension – *Meeting Peggy Sue*

1. Every Sunday they would go sailing.
2. First of all he felt **moody/upset**. Later, he **realised his dream buying the boat** because **he'd never had dared to do it before**.
3. Redundancy money; savings and sale of the car.
4. It builds up a sense of wonder and excitement.
5. Amazed, Shocked.

Page 49 – Reading comprehension – *The Owl and the Pussycat*

1. Pea green – *both needed for mark.*
2. A five pound note.
3. A year and a day.
4. Any two of: boat/note; above/love; honey/money.
5. Any two of: sing to each other; say how beautiful they are; get married; dance; sail away together; hold hands.
6. Any three of: an owl/bird and cat sail away to get married; a turkey marries them; they get a ring off a pig; they dance together; they eat honey; owl plays a guitar.

Pages 51–52 – Reading comprehension – *Sky Lords*

1.

Meaning	Word from Day and night
A bird which hunts and eats other animals.	bird of prey
Sharp claws on the birds' feet.	talons
An animal which the bird wants to eat.	prey
A bird which uses its feet to grab other animals it wants to eat.	raptor

   1 mark for two correct answers; 2 marks for all four answers correct.

2. Swoop.
3. Rip.
4. So they can look down on the snakes; so they get extra power to stamp on snakes; so they can escape being bitten by snakes.
5. **Bold**: subheadings, to separate the information; *Italic*: names of the birds.
6. It gives facts about birds. (*1 mark*) It splits up the information with headings. (*1 mark*)
7. It can catch a mouse in total darkness by hearing alone.

Pages 55–56 – Reading comprehension – *Thunderbird*

1. Before – Near the sea. After – On the grassland or the prairie.
2. Beat.
3. 3, 5, 6, 2, 4, 1.
4. Whales.
5. To make it sound like the storm went on for a very, very long time.
6.

The question people asked about the world	The answer in the legend
What makes strong winds?	Thunderbird's wings flapping.
What makes lightning?	Thunderbird's eyes opening and closing.
What makes thunder?	Thunderbird's wings flapping.

   3 correct = 3 marks, 2 correct = 2 marks and 1 correct = 1 mark.
7. Any three from: made thunder; wind and lightning; brought them food; saved their lives; had supernatural powers and strength.
   Also allow the fact that the legend has been passed on for generations – still remember the thunderbird today.

Commas

A comma is a punctuation mark that separates a part of a sentence. Commas are used:
- to separate names, adjectives or items in a list –
  They took crisps, sandwiches and a bottle of lemonade to the park.
  OR
  Bobby, George, Dennis and Alex were all members of the winning team.
  Notice that you don't need a comma before the last item in the list. Use 'and' instead.
- to give extra information – *Mr Cooper, my teacher, is leaving next week.*
- after a subordinate clause – *In spite of the number of guards, he still managed to escape.*

Try saying a sentence out loud before you write it down. It will help you to 'hear' where the commas should go.

Tip	★ When you join two equal clauses in a compound sentence using *and, but* or *so* you do not need a comma, e.g. *Mr Timms' class play chess on Tuesday and Mrs Kelly's class play it on Friday.*
	NOT: *Mr Timms' class play chess on Tuesday, and Mrs Kelly's class play it on Friday.*

Rewrite these sentences adding the commas.

1 Broccoli cabbage spinach and carrots are all full of vitamins.

_____

_____

2 A simple healthy snack can be a few nuts seeds raw vegetables or fruit.

_____

_____

3 For a delicious healthy drink mix some squeezed raspberries blueberries and a banana with some yoghurt or milk.

_____

_____

4 Some foods contain a lot of fat salt or sugar so remember to eat them in moderation.

_____

_____

Speech punctuation

Direct speech

Using direct speech means that you use the speaker's actual words inside speech marks (' ').

To finish the spoken words, the most common punctuation is a comma used at the end of the spoken words INSIDE the speech marks.

If the speaker continues talking, you need another comma before the next spoken words.

If you start the sentence with the speaker and speech verb, the comma comes before the first speech mark and the speech begins with a capital letter.

Full stops, exclamation marks and question marks must be placed inside the speech marks.

And finally DON'T FORGET– new speaker = new line.

Tips	★ Notice that when the speech verb comes in the middle of one continuous sentence, the second group of words inside speech marks does <u>not</u> need a capital letter at the beginning.
	★ The speech verb or pronoun after the spoken words always begins with a lowercase letter, while a PROPER NOUN begins with a capital.

Practice question
Rewrite this conversation by putting in all the correct speech punctuation. Only the full stops and capital letters have been included.

Don't forget to add commas, question marks or exclamation marks as well as the speech marks. And don't forget – new speaker = new line.

Have you seen my glasses called Granny from the sitting room.

I could just hear her voice so I called back Did you say something Granny.

I went downstairs to find out. What did you say I asked.

I can't find my glasses she replied Will you help me find them. It's such a nuisance. Granny dear I laughed Look in the mirror. They're on your head.

Oh silly me she laughed.

Apostrophes

Apostrophes to show possession

We use apostrophes to show that something belongs to somebody (possession).
The cat's pyjamas!

Remember – if the noun is plural the apostrophe moves.
The cats' pyjamas!

Apostrophes to show omission

We also use apostrophes to show that a letter has been missed out (omission).
Did not becomes *didn't.*

Tips	★ Remember the rule about **it**! An apostrophe is only ever used to show omission, i.e. *It is a lovely day* becomes *It's a lovely day.* ★ Never use an apostrophe with **it** to show possession, i.e. *I cannot find its collar.*

Practice questions
Write 'P' for possession or 'O' for omission to show the purpose of the apostrophes in these sentences.

1 The ship's biscuits were full of weevils. _____

2 Jack was sorry that he didn't see the last episode of the serial. _____

3 The pupils' work was of a high standard in the tests. _____

4 We wouldn't like to be late for the show! _____

5 It's been a very long day! _____

Rewrite these sentences using an apostrophe showing possession.

(1) Donnas shoes were covered in mud.

_____

(2) Take your chairs and put them in Mr Browns classroom.

_____

(3) The parrots feathers were blue and red. *(singular)*

_____

(4) The soldiers boots were highly polished. *(plural)*

_____

(5) The sailors clothes were crumpled. *(singular)*

_____

Rewrite these sentences by shortening the verbs and using apostrophes of omission.

(1) I can not finish my story yet.

_____

(2) You have not been swimming for ages.

_____

(3) Your mum would not like to see you looking so grubby.

_____

(4) This skateboard has not got alloy wheels.

_____

(5) Tom is not a good runner.

_____

Can you rewrite this sentence with an apostrophe of omission?

Can you not make a louder noise than that?

Test your punctuation

This passage has had all the punctuation taken out. Your challenge is to rewrite the passage below putting in the correct punctuation. The number of capital letters, full stops, commas, question marks, exclamation marks, apostrophes and sets of speech marks is given beneath the passage. Can you find the correct home for them all?

Read through the passage before you start and try to 'hear' it in your head. Remember, punctuation gives a 'voice' to your writing.

the children made a lot of noise as they approached through the wood

were tramping through the woods they sang were tramping through the fields their voices let us know they were coming so we built up the camp fire and began to heat up the beans and sausages we knew they would be hungry after the hike

here you are at last I shouted as soon as the first boy who I think was called daniel appeared through the trees quickly followed by four others they looked bedraggled but happy

did you enjoy that i asked

yeah they all yelled it was great

soon frank jenkins appeared bringing up the rear he beckoned to me and muttered solemnly in my ear im afraid theres been a problem

Punctuation marks missing	
Capital letters	19
Full stops	9
Commas	8
Question marks	1
Exclamation marks	3
Apostrophes	3
Sets of speech marks	7

Vocabulary

Choose your words carefully … Knowing how to spell lots of words is not much use unless you know how to use them. 'Variety' is the spice of life – and a varied vocabulary improves your writing!

Simile

A simile is where a writer has compared the subject to something else. Usually the writer will use *like* or *as*, e.g. *As brave as a lion* or *he runs like the wind*.

Invent similes for the following.

Tip	★ **Lots of similes are over-used and so are not very interesting, e.g. *as black as coal, as quick as a flash*. Try to make up ones of your own.**

1. clouds	**2.** yellow
3. long hair	**4.** birdsong
5. jumping	**6.** daisies
7. kicking a ball	**8.** sleep
9. a bowl of beans	**10.** a strict teacher

Metaphor

A metaphor is when the writer writes about something as if it was really something else, e.g. *He is dynamite. Every goal he scores is explosive!*

Write your own sentences containing these metaphors.

1 winter's frozen grip

_____

_____

2 lace petals

_____

_____

3 the golden boy

_____

_____

4 a net of stars

_____

_____

5 blanket of fog

_____

_____

6 the tree's bony fingers

_____

_____

Personification

Personification is a type of metaphor. It is when the writer gives non-human objects or ideas human characteristics.

Example:

The drain gurgled with satisfaction as the keys disappeared through the grate.

Describe these nouns using personification.

1. autumn leaves	2. a river
3. an old bus	4. a camera
5. a mountain	6. a poem

Nouns and verbs

Choosing accurate nouns and powerful verbs can sometimes improve your writing more than just adding adjectives and adverbs.

Make these sentences more interesting by choosing better nouns and verbs.

(1) The tree shook in the wind.

_____

(2) The team was very pleased when it won.

_____

(3) Lots of people saw the parade.

_____

(4) 'Go and get another book,' she said quietly.

_____

Adjectives

Use adjectives to help your reader get a clear picture of what you mean, e.g. _an ugly crowd_ is very different from _a jubilant crowd_.

Add an adjective to the words in the first column to create a happy mood, to the second to create a sad mood and to the third to create a scary mood.

[ ]	face	[ ]	face	[ ]	face
[ ]	speech	[ ]	speech	[ ]	speech
[ ]	touch	[ ]	touch	[ ]	touch
[ ]	wind	[ ]	wind	[ ]	wind

Adverbs

An adverb can clarify the meaning of a verb. Sometimes adverbs can be phrases, e.g. *ran like the wind*. Do not use adverbs that mean the same as the verb, e.g. *whispered quietly*.

Write two sentences for each verb but use a different adverb in each sentence. Notice how the meaning changes.

	Sentence 1	Sentence 2
jumped		
stared		
floated		
rode		
curled		

Alliteration

Using words with the same initial sound can improve your writing, e.g. *He wearily watched as they left.*

Add an alliterative adjective to these sentences.

1 The [   ] trees were whipped by the wind.

2 Her [   ] tongue spat out the words.

Add an alliterative adverb to these sentences.

1 She [   ] heard the sound.

2 Kurt [   ] strode across the room.

Spelling

The next four pages have a number of spelling lists, spelling rules and spelling games. You will already know some words but you may be unsure of the meaning of others. It would be really useful to learn how to spell all of these words and with time spent learning them – a little and often is best – there is no reason why you can't.

Look, Say, Cover, Write and Check

The tried and tested method of 'Look, Say, Cover, Write and Check' works very well for most people, so give it a go.

Look at the word on the page.

Say the word in your head or out loud.

Cover the word with your hand.

Write the word.

Check the word by lifting your hand.

Mnemonics

Another way to remember spellings is by using mnemonics. A mnemonic is a silly way of remembering something. Take the word 'C O U G H'. Each letter can stand for a new word in an easy-to-remember phrase.

Colds	C
Open	O
Up	U
Green	G
Hankies!	H

This is a useful way of remembering how to spell tricky words or those words that, for some reason, you keep getting wrong.

Learning to spell new words is not much use on its own. When you can spell a new word correctly, make sure you are aware of what it means and try to use it in your writing. This will give your written work more power and, at the same time, widen your vocabulary, so you can express yourself more freely.

Spelling lists

List 1
Here is a list of the 100 most common words. You probably know most or all of them already. Don't go any further until you can spell each one correctly!

the	with	much	been	are
as	your	to	how	have
not	write	this	good	when
may	colour	we	place	their
each	tree	other	that	use
up	has	what	he	out
no	about	its	if	could
because	then	first	were	new
of	water	went	into	you
or	like	over	number	which
Mum	a	people	him	but
Dad	on	in	through	many
draw	they	by	it	do
can	I	his	from	only
there	should	some	an	any
two	dog	than	had	make
such	cat	would	them	be
must	climb	very	made	one
see	time	more	same	these
and	also	under	work	so

Spelling lists

List 2
Here is another list of key words. You should have learned these by the end of Year 4. Now's the chance to see if you did. Don't go any further until you have!

above	every	morning	sometimes	under
across	following	near	started	until
almost before	found	never	still	upon
began	goes	often	stopped	used
being	gone	only	such	walk
below	heard	other	think	watch
better	high	outside	though	while
between	inside	place	thought	without
change	jumped	right	today	woke
coming	knew	round	together	write
didn't	know	second	told	year
different	leave	show	tries	young
does	might			

Spelling lists

List 3
Here is a list of words that aren't spelled the way they sound. Most don't follow any of the regular spelling rules so often catch out many people. Learn them all. If you get stuck on one or two, then think of a mnemonic to help you remember.

beautiful	aeroplane	listen	thought	autumn
business	encyclopaedia	which	weight	except
scream	machine	lacy	February	jewellery
dream	nation	scary	library	write
height	special	laugh	address	wreck
minute	whistle			

List your mnemonics here

Reviewing your work

Rereading or reviewing your work is an important part of being a writer. No writer thinks their work is finished without rereading it and checking it makes sense. Don't worry if you find things that need changing – there are always changes to be made. It is a good opportunity to look at ways in which your writing could be improved.

Here are some ideas to keep in mind when you are reviewing your work.

★ **Make sure your reader will understand your main message**. For example, if you are writing a mystery story, will your reader want to find out what happens? Ask yourself if you have given too many clues to the ending. Is there a feeling of suspense and excitement? If you are writing an explanation, have you used connectives to help your reader follow the process that you are explaining? Would you be able to understand the explanation easily? If you are not sure, have another look at the guidelines for writing explanations.

★ **Make sure you have followed the guidelines for the text type you are writing.** If you are not sure, go back and check. Keep the style constant and try not to slip from one type of writing to another. If you have started in the first person voice, have you kept to it all the way through your writing? Have you kept to the same verb tense? Don't get worried if you find mistakes – just correct them and try to remember for the future. No one gets it right all the time, but reviewing your work helps you to spot the errors that could lose you marks.

★ **Check your spelling and grammar.** Look carefully as you read and, if a word doesn't look right, try it out a few times on a piece of paper. If you can, look it up in a dictionary and try to learn the correct spelling for the future. Read your sentences aloud. This will help you to hear when something doesn't sound right. When you think your grammar is not quite right, try saying the sentence in different ways and rewrite it a few times. Pick the one that you think sounds best and don't be afraid to make changes. Go back and check for any simple mistakes. Have you added all your capital letters and full stops?

Writers' tip

Read as often as you can. Reading helps you to become familiar with good writing, helps you to remember patterns and helps you to learn how to structure your sentences. Read as many kinds of books as you can. This will help you to get ideas for your own writing.

Keep a notebook and write down ideas, phrases, sentences and words that you like. If you read a phrase that might be useful, don't be afraid to make use of it. You can learn a lot from other writers' ideas. Jot them down in your writer's notebook. You never know when they might come in handy.

Writing and reading skills

Did you know that teachers are helping you develop your **writing** in at least eight ways? These are called 'assessment focuses' (AFs) and they are described here.

AF	Teacher language	This means...
1	Write imaginative, interesting and thoughtful texts	My writing is imaginative, interesting and thoughtful
2	Produce texts which are appropriate to the task, reader and purpose	I am able to write for different purposes and audiences according to the task set
3	Organise and present whole texts effectively, sequencing and structuring information, ideas and events	I can plan my writing and produce texts that sequence ideas, information and events within an appropriate structure
4	Construct paragraphs and use cohesion within and between paragraphs	I can use topic sentences and linking sentences to guide my reader through the text
5	Vary sentences for clarity, purpose and effect	I can use different types of sentences – simple, compound and complex – according to purpose and to create specific effects
6	Write with technical accuracy of syntax and punctuation in phrases, clauses and sentences	I am able to use different types of punctuation to make the meaning clear to my reader
7	Select appropriate and effective vocabulary	I can select and use a range of vocabulary, making choices according to purpose and audience
8	Use correct spelling	I can spell accurately

Reading is not just about being able to say and understand the words you see. Reading skills include the different ways you are expected to respond to a text. The seven assessment focuses for reading are:

AF	Teacher language	This means...
1	Use a range of strategies, including accurate decoding of text, to read for meaning	I can read for meaning
2	Understand, describe, select or retrieve information, events or ideas from texts and use quotations and references from texts	I can understand and pick out the appropriate quote, event or idea from a text and use PEE (Point, Evidence, Explain) to demonstrate my understanding
3	Deduce, infer or interpret information, events or ideas from texts	I can read and understand meaning that is only hinted at
4	Identify and comment on the structure and organisation of texts, including grammatical and presentational features at text level	I can identify the text type according to its presentational features and conventions. I can also comment on the writer's choice of text type to suit purpose
5	Explain and comment on the writer's use of language, including grammatical and literary features at word and sentence level	I can explain why the writer has made certain language choices (imperative verbs, emotive language, figurative language, formal/informal etc.)
6	Identify and comment on writers' purposes and viewpoints and the overall effect of a text on the reader	I can identify the writer's purpose and viewpoint and comment on how this affects the reader
7	Relate texts to their social, cultural and historical contexts and literary traditions	I can see how texts fit into their cultural and historical traditions

Reading comprehension

Answering different types of questions

The reading test consists of different types of questions. Some of them are easy to answer (the information is right there) and some require you to apply some higher-level thinking skills. These are the Level 5 questions and when you look in the margin for the number of marks, they are usually worth 2 or 3.

Do not let a box with lots of lines to write your answers in put you off. If you think you could try to answer the question, even if you only write two lines, you may get 1 mark. Some of these questions involve comparing the texts you have read in the booklet, e.g. if there was a story, a poem and non-fiction and the question asks you if the booklet title was a good title for the booklet you need to say why it was good for the story, why it was good for the poem **and** why it was good for the non-fiction.

Some questions ask you how effective a particular word or phrase is, e.g. *On page 7 the author writes ' there wasn't a single football fan singing as the referee pointed to the penalty spot'. Why is this an effective way of describing the football fans reaction?*

If you write 'because it's effective', you are repeating the question. Be careful not to do this.

If you write 'because he uses good description', this is a little vague and you will need to expand your understanding and explain how 'not a single fan' emphasises that all of the fans reacted in the same way to the referee's decision.

This table will help you to recognise the question types and identify how to answer them.

Type of question	How to recognise them	Skills needed
Literal	Who, what, when?	Answer is usually right there in text
Inference	Why, how?	'Read between the lines', what is hinted at
Deduction	Do you think?	Find evidence, clues to support you
Evaluation	Explain why…	Explain what makes something effective, successful, etc…
Authorial intent	The author uses… What is the effect of this?	Explain why the writer made these choices

Sometimes you may need to quote from the reading booklet to support your answer. For example:

I know that Miss Wileman is wealthy because it says in the text *'She had money coming out of her ears and for Miss Wileman, money really did grow on trees!'*

About the Reading Test

The Reading Test comes in the form of two booklets – one containing the texts you will read and another for your answers.

You have one hour to read the booklets and answer all the questions.

Reading the texts

Read the text in the booklet. DON'T RUSH. Make sure you read the contents page; it has key information which prepares you for the types of texts you will be reading, for example *A country of colour* – a brief summary of how South Africa has changed in recent years.

> Always read the question carefully before you write. Look at the top of the page; it will tell you which section of the reading booklet you need to look at.

If there are words you don't understand, read on and perhaps the paragraph will make sense anyway.

Answering the questions

After you have read the question, look across in the margin and you will see how many marks the question is worth (these usually range from 1 to 3 marks). This should help you to structure your answer. You must REFER TO THE TEXT in your answers – you can read the reading booklet as many times as you want! Although some of the questions require deep thinking, the answers will always relate to the reading booklet.

There are different types of questions which you will begin to recognise:
- Some questions require a short answer, for example *who, what, when* style questions.
- Some questions require a longer answer, for example *why, how, do you think* questions.
- Some questions involve no writing at all, but instead you will need to circle the right answer, tick some boxes or match up ideas.
- You might be asked to comment on why an author has used a particular word or phrase.
- You could be asked about how a text is organised, for example pictures, subheadings, text in boxes, bold print, etc.
- Some questions ask for your opinions and views – remember to link these to the text.

Now you can begin to answer the questions. Remember to REFER TO THE TEXT. You do not need to answer any questions from memory.

Achieving Level 4 reading

At Level 4, you show that you can understand a range of texts and understand their ideas, themes, events and characters. You show that you are beginning to use inference and deduction to read between the lines and can bring your own experiences into your understanding. You refer to the text when explaining your views. You can find and use ideas and information from different parts of a text.

If you can do all of these, you will achieve Level 4 and even Level 5!

Meeting Peggy Sue

These questions are about the opening pages of *Kensuke's Kingdom* by Michael Morpurgo.

Michael's life seemed fine. His Mum and Dad were happy and every Sunday all of them, plus their dog Lucky, would go sailing in their small boat. Then, when Michael was 11, his parents were made redundant (lost their jobs). His Dad changed, became moody and life wasn't fine any more. Dad sold their car and left to find them somewhere else to make a new life. A week later, he phoned to tell them he had found a place. Mum, Michael and Lucky packed their cases and travelled to Fareham, a town on the south coast. As this extract begins Mum, Dad, Michael and Lucky are walking alongside the water.

'What are we doing here?' my mother asked.

'There's someone I want you to meet. A good friend of mine. She's called Peggy Sue. She's been looking forward to meeting you. I've told her all about you.'

My mother frowned at me in puzzlement. I wasn't any the wiser either. All I knew for certain was that he was being deliberately mysterious.

We struggled on with our suitcases, the gulls crying overhead, the yacht masts flapping around us, and Lucky yapping at all of it, until at last he stopped right by a gang plank that led up to a gleaming dark-blue yacht. He put the cases down and turned to face us. He was grinning from ear to ear.

'Here she is,' he said. 'Let me introduce you. This is the Peggy Sue. Our new home. Well?'

Considering everything, my mother took it pretty well. She didn't shout at him. She just went very quiet, and she stayed quiet all through his explanation down in the galley-kitchen over a cup of tea.

'It wasn't a spur-of-the-moment thing, you know. I've been thinking about it a long time, all those years working in the factory. All right, maybe I was just dreaming about it in those days. Funny when you think about it: if I hadn't lost my job, I'd never have dared do it, not in a million years.' He knew he wasn't making much sense. 'All right, then. Here's what I thought. What is it that we all love doing most? Sailing, right? Wouldn't it be wonderful, I thought, if we could just take off and sail around the world? There are people who've done it. Blue water sailing, they call it. I've read about it in the magazines.

'Like I said, it was just a dream to start with. And then, no job and no chance of a job. I was so miserable, so depressed. But then I thought... We've got our redundancy money, what little there was of it. There's a bit saved up, and the car money. Not a fortune, but enough. What to do with it? I could put it all in the bank, like the others did. But what for? Just to watch it dribble away till there was nothing left? Or, I thought, I could do something really special with it, a once-in-a-lifetime thing: we could sail around the world. Africa. South America. Australia. The Pacific. We could see places we've only ever dreamed of.'

We sat there, completely dumbstruck.

Tips	★ **Read the text twice, then read the questions twice before you begin to answer.**
	★ **Look at how many marks each question has.**
	★ **Look back at page 45 to remind yourself of what you need to do. If you do all this, you can achieve Level 4!**

If you need more space for your answers use extra paper.

1 What did Michael's family do together every Sunday?

2 Complete the sentences to explain the different feelings that Michael's father had about losing his job.

First of all, he felt [   ] . Later, he

[   ] because

[   ] before.

3 Give **three** ways that explain how Michael's Dad got the money to buy the boat.

4 *'Africa. South America. Australia. The Pacific.'* What is the effect of Michael's father using these short sentences?

5 Tick **two** words which show how Michael and his Mum react to the idea of sailing round the world.

| Nervous ☐ | Shocked ☐ | Frightened ☐ |
| Scared ☐ | Amazed ☐ | Angry ☐ |

Total marks [   ]

The Owl and the Pussycat

These questions are about *The Owl and the Pussycat* by Edward Lear.

The Owl and the Pussy-cat went to sea
　　In a beautiful pea green boat,
They took some honey, and plenty of money,
　　Wrapped up in a five pound note.
The Owl looked up to the stars above,
　　And sang to a small guitar,
'O lovely Pussy! O Pussy my love,
　　What a beautiful Pussy you are,
　　　　You are,
　　　　You are!
What a beautiful Pussy you are!'

Pussy said to the Owl, 'You elegant fowl!
　　How charmingly sweet you sing!
O let us be married! too long we have tarried:
　　But what shall we do for a ring?'
They sailed away, for a year and a day,
　　To the land where the Bong-tree grows
And there in a wood a Piggy-wig stood
　　With a ring at the end of his nose,
　　　　His nose,
　　　　His nose,
With a ring at the end of his nose.

'Dear pig, are you willing to sell for one shilling
　　Your ring?' Said the Piggy, 'I will.'
So they took it away, and were married next day
　　By the Turkey who lives on the hill.
They dined on mince, and slices of quince,
　　Which they ate with a runcible spoon;
And hand in hand, on the edge of the sand,
　　They danced by the light of the moon,
　　　　The moon,
　　　　The moon,
They danced by the light of the moon.

Glossary

tarried – waited

quince – a fruit resembling a pear

runcible spoon – a long handled spoon with a large curved bowl

Tips	★ Read the poem at least twice, then read the questions twice before you begin to answer.
	★ Look at how many marks each question has.
	★ Look back at page 45 to remind yourself of what you need to do. If you do all this, you can achieve Level 4!

If you need more space for your answers use extra paper.

1 Give **two** words from the poem that describe the boat.

AF2

1

1 mark

2 What was the honey and money wrapped in?

AF2

2

1 mark

3 How long did the Owl and the Pussycat sail for?

AF2

3

1 mark

4 Edward Lear uses rhyme in this poem. Underline **two** words which rhyme in the extract below:

The Owl and the Pussy-cat went to sea

   In a beautiful pea green boat,

They took some honey, and plenty of money,

   Wrapped up in a five pound note.

The Owl looked up to the stars above,

   And sang to a small guitar,

'O lovely Pussy! O Pussy my love,

AF4

4

1 mark

5 Give **two** ways you can tell that the Owl and the Pussycat love one another.

AF3

5

2 marks

6 Give **three** reasons why this poem could be called a 'nonsense poem'.

AF7

6

3 marks

Total marks

49

Sky Lords

Read the information below about birds of prey and answer the questions that follow.

Day and night

Birds of prey are birds which have to kill and eat other animals to live. Some, like falcons, hunt in the daytime; others, like owls, hunt at night. Some live near the sea or lakes so they can catch fish. Others live near mountains so they can swoop down and catch small animals. You can even see birds of prey in towns or near motorways, hunting for mice on grass verges or in parks and gardens.

But all these birds of prey use the same deadly weapons for hunting: strong, sharp claws called 'talons', and a powerful, hooked beak. Sometimes birds of prey are called 'raptors', which means that they catch their prey by seizing it in their talons. Once a raptor has its talons in its prey, the creature has little chance of surviving as the raptor will not let go. It will then use its curved beak to rip the meat into bits small enough to swallow.

All eyes and ears

Raptors which hunt by day have amazing eyesight. An eagle soaring high above the ground may be a speck to us, but it, looking down from above, can clearly see a tiny mouse moving in the grass below. Owls hunt by night and have enormous eyes, designed to pick up as much light as possible when it is dark. However, the owl cannot see detail very well. It makes up for this with superb hearing. An owl's hearing is so good that scientists have found it can catch a mouse in total darkness by hearing alone.

Fussy eaters

Some raptors catch and eat particular animals, and their bodies and beaks are shaped to help them. The *Snail Kite* in America lives on a diet of water snails! Its beak has a particularly long curved hook, so it is able to remove the snail from its shell before eating it. The *Secretary Bird* in Africa has much longer legs than other raptors. Like all raptors, it kills with its feet – but it does not swoop onto its prey. Instead this bird stamps on it, with deadly force and accuracy. They are famous for killing and eating snakes.

Rulers of the sky

The *Great Horned Owl* from North, Central and South America is sometimes called 'the tiger of the woods'. It can kill prey up to three times its size, such as foxes. But all around the world, the eagle is seen as the king of birds. The eagle was chosen by the Romans as a noble, strong bird to represent them. It appeared on their standards, carried into battles. More recently, the *Bald Eagle* was chosen as the national emblem of the United States. Look out for it on TV when the President makes a speech.

Tips
★ Read the text at least twice. Then read the questions twice before you begin to answer.
★ Look at how many marks each question has.
★ Look back at page 45 to remind yourself of what you need to do. If you do all this, you can achieve Level 4!

If you need more space for your answers use extra paper.

1 Complete this table to show the meanings of words used in the section **Day and night**. One has been done for you.

Meaning	Word from Day and night
A bird which hunts and eats other animals.	
Sharp claws on the birds' feet.	
An animal which the bird wants to eat.	**prey**
A bird which uses its feet to grab other animals it wants to eat.	

AF2

1

2 marks

2 Find and copy **one** word in the section **Day and night** which tells you that the birds fly down smoothly and quickly.

AF5

2

1 mark

3 Find and copy **one** word in the section **Day and night** which tells you that the birds tear the meat into thin pieces.

AF5

3

1 mark

4 Give **three** reasons why you think it might be helpful for the Secretary Bird to have such very long legs.

AF3

4

3 marks

5 Throughout this text some words have been written in **bold** or *italics*. Explain why you think this is.

Bold: _____

Italic: _____

AF2

5

2 marks

6 This extract has been taken from an information book. Tick **two** features which help us to identify this.

It is written in the first person. ☐

It gives facts about birds. ☐

It is written in chronological order. ☐

It is written in note form. ☐

It splits up the information with headings. ☐

It tells a story about birds. ☐

AF4, 5

6

2 marks

7 In the section **All eyes and ears** we learn about some of the amazing things that birds of prey can do. How have scientists proved that an owl has excellent hearing?

AF2

7

1 mark

Total marks

Thunderbird

This is a legend told by a Native American tribe, the Quillayute tribe. Read the information below about Native American legends and answer the questions that follow.

Long ago, there was a sad time in the land of the Quillayute people. For day after day, week after week, month after month, great storms blew. Rain and hail and then sleet and snow, came down upon the land. The hailstones were so large that many people were killed. Storms rocked the ocean so the fishermen could not go out in their canoes to catch the fish and whales which the tribe used to live on. The people had to leave their villages near the sea and move to the great grassland, the prairie.

Here, without their usual food, the people grew thin and weak from hunger. The hailstones beat down the plants which gave them nuts or berries. Ice locked the rivers so the men could not fish. Soon, the people had eaten all the grass and roots on the prairie. There was no food left. As children died without food, even the strongest and bravest of their fathers could do nothing. They called upon the Great Spirit for help, but no help came.

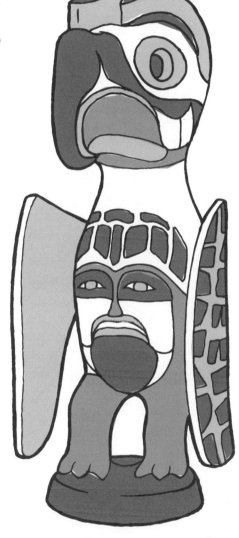

At last the Great Chief of the Quillayute called a meeting of his people. He was old and wise.

'Take comfort, my people,' the Chief said. 'We will call again upon the Great Spirit for help. If no help comes, then we will know it is His will that we die. If it is not His will that we live, then we will die bravely, as brave Quillayute have always died. Let us talk with the Great Spirit.'

So the weak and hungry people sat in silence while the Chief talked with the Great Spirit, who had looked kindly upon the Quillayute for hundreds of years.

When his prayer had ended, the Chief turned again to his people. 'Now we will wait for the will of the One who is wise and all-powerful.'

The people waited. No one spoke. There was nothing but silence and darkness. Suddenly, there came a great noise, and flashes of lightning cut the darkness. A deep whirring sound, like giant wings beating, came from the place of the setting sun. All of the people turned to gaze toward the sky above the ocean as a huge, bird-shaped creature flew towards them.

This bird was larger than any they had ever seen. His wings, from tip to tip, were twice as long as a war canoe. Each feather was as long as a canoe paddle. He had a huge, curving beak and his eyes glowed like fire. When he flapped his wings, he made thunder and a great wind. When he opened and shut his eyes, he made lightning.

The people saw that his great claws held a giant whale.

In silence, they watched while Thunderbird – for so the bird was named by everyone – carefully lowered the whale to the ground before them. Thunderbird then flew high in the sky and went back to his home, a cave high in the mountains.

Thunderbird had saved the Quillayute from dying. The people knew that the Great Spirit had heard their prayer and sent them food. Even today, they never forget that visit from Thunderbird, never forget that it ended long days of hunger and death. For on the prairie near their village are big, round stones that the grandfathers say are the hardened hailstones of that storm long ago.

Tips	★ Read the text twice, then read the questions twice before you begin to answer.
	★ Look at how many marks each question has.
	★ Look back at page 45 to remind yourself of what you need to do. If you do all this, you can achieve Level 4!

If you need more space for your answers use extra paper.

1 Where did the Quillayute people have their villages **before** the terrible storms came?

> [ ]

Where did they live **after** the storms?

> [ ]

AF2

[ ] 1

2 marks

2 Find and copy **one** word which tells you that the hail fell very hard and violently onto the plants.

> [ ]

AF5

[ ] 2

1 mark

3 Number these events 1 to 6, in the order they happen in the story. Two have been done for you.

The old, wise chief prayed to the Great Spirit for help.	
The Quillayute people could eat and were saved from death.	
Even today the Quillayute people remember Thunderbird's visit.	
The people started to starve to death because they had no food.	**2**
Thunderbird came, bringing a whale in his claws.	
Terrible storms forced the Quillayute people to leave their homes.	**1**

AF3

[ ] 3

2 marks

4 Draw a circle around the food which the Quillayute people used to eat before the storms came. One has already been done for you as an example.

hailstones   whales   berries   grass   (fish)

AF3

[ ] 4

1 mark

5 *For day after day, week after week, month after month, great storms blew.*

Why did the writer repeat the word 'after' three times in this sentence?

Choose and tick the **best** answer.

To show that weeks are longer than days during the storm	
To make it sound like the storm went on for a very, very long time	
To make it clear one day came after another during the storm	
To show the storm lasted more than a week	

AF5

5

1 mark

6 This story is a legend, told by Native American people for hundreds of years, to answer questions about the world around them. Fill in the missing question and answers.

The question people asked about the world	The answer in the legend
What makes strong winds?	
	Thunderbird's eyes opening and closing.
	Thunderbird's wings flapping.

AF7

6

3 marks

7 In legends there is usually a hero. Explain **three** ways in which the Thunderbird was a hero for the Quillayute people.

AF6

7

3 marks

Total marks